Finding Life's Purpose

Inspiration for young people

with
Pope Benedict XVI

*All booklets are published thanks to the
generous support of the members of the
Catholic Truth Society*

CATHOLIC TRUTH SOCIETY
PUBLISHERS TO THE HOLY SEE

Contents

Happiness comes from friendship with God 3

Discover the purpose of your lives 9

Radiate Christ's love to all 13

Making the best of school and study 22

Turn to the Saints 27

The texts of the first three chapters are drawn from addresses of His Holiness Pope Benedict XVI at Twickenham, 17 September 2010, Westminster Cathedral Piazza and Hyde Park, London, 18 September 2010.

Happiness comes from friendship with God

It is not often that a Pope, or indeed anyone else, has the opportunity to speak to the students of all the Catholic schools of England, Wales and Scotland at the same time. And since I have the chance now, there is something I very much want to say to you. I hope that among those of you listening to me today there are some of the future saints of the twenty-first century. What God wants most of all for each one of you is that you should become holy. He loves you much more than you could ever begin to imagine, and he wants the very best for you. And by far the best thing for you is to grow in holiness.

Who do you want to be?

Perhaps some of you have never thought about this before. Perhaps some of you think being a saint is not for you. Let me explain what I mean. When we are young, we can usually think of people that we look up to, people we admire, people we want to be like. It could be someone we meet in our daily lives that we hold in great esteem. Or it could be someone famous. We live in a celebrity culture, and young people are often encouraged to model themselves on figures from the world of sport or entertainment. My question for you is this: what are the qualities you see in others that you would most like to have yourselves? What kind of person would you really like to be?

Where will you find happiness?

When I invite you to become saints, I am asking you not to be content with second best. I am asking you not to pursue one limited goal and ignore all the others. Having money makes it possible to be generous and to do good in the world, but on its own, it is not enough to make us happy. Being highly skilled in some activity or profession is good, but it will not satisfy us unless we aim for something greater still. It might make us famous, but it will not make us happy. Happiness is something we all want, but one of the great tragedies in this world is that so many people never find it, because they look for it in the wrong places. The key to it is very simple – true happiness is to be found in God. We need to have the courage to place our deepest hopes in God alone, not in money, in a career, in worldly success, or in our relationships with others, but in God. Only he can satisfy the deepest needs of our hearts.

When do things really start to change in life?

Not only does God love us with a depth and an intensity that we can scarcely begin to comprehend, but he invites us to respond to that love. You all know what it is like when you meet someone interesting and attractive, and you want to be that person's friend. You always hope they will find you interesting and attractive, and want to be your friend. God wants your friendship. And once you enter into friendship with God, everything in your life begins to change. As you come to know him better, you find you want to reflect something of his infinite goodness in your own life. You are attracted to the practice of virtue. You begin to see greed and selfishness and all the other sins for what they really are, destructive and dangerous tendencies that cause deep suffering and do great damage, and you want to avoid falling into that trap yourselves. You begin to feel compassion for people in difficulties and you are eager to do something to help them. You want to come to the aid of the poor and the hungry, you want to comfort the sorrowful, you want to be kind and generous. And once these things begin to matter to you, you are well on the way to becoming saints.

Friendship with God brings real happiness

In your Catholic schools, there is always a bigger picture over and above the individual subjects you study, the different skills you learn. All the work you do is placed in the context of growing in friendship with God, and all that flows from that friendship. So you learn not just to be good students, but good citizens, good people. As you move higher up the school, you have to make choices regarding the subjects you study; you begin to specialize with a view to what you are going to do later on in life. That is right and proper. But always remember that every subject you study is part of a bigger picture. Never allow yourselves to become narrow. The world needs good scientists, but a scientific outlook becomes dangerously narrow if it ignores the religious or ethical dimension of life, just as religion becomes narrow if it rejects the legitimate contribution of science to our understanding of the world. We need good historians and philosophers and economists, but if the account they give of human life within their particular field is too narrowly focused, they can lead us seriously astray.

Practice virtue and grow in knowledge of God

A good school provides a rounded education for the whole person. And a good Catholic school, over and above this, should help all its students to become saints. I know that there are many non-Catholics studying in the Catholic schools in Great Britain, and I wish to include all of you in my words today. I pray that you too will feel encouraged to practise virtue and to grow in knowledge and friendship with God alongside your Catholic classmates. You are a reminder to them of the bigger picture that exists outside the school, and indeed, it is only right that respect and friendship for members of other religious traditions should be among the virtues learned in a Catholic school. I hope too that you will want to share with everyone you meet the values and insights you have learned through the Christian education you have received.

Dear friends, I thank you for your attention, I promise to pray for you, and I ask you to pray for me.

Discover the purpose of your lives

In these few moments that we are together, I wish to speak to you from my own heart, and I ask you to open your hearts to what I have to say.

Look into your heart

I ask each of you, first and foremost, to look into your own heart. Think of all the love that your heart was made to receive, and all the love it is meant to give. After all, we were made for love. This is what the Bible means when it says that we are made in the image and likeness of God: we were made to know the God of love, the God who is Father, Son and Holy Spirit, and to find our supreme fulfilment in that divine love that knows no beginning or end.

Love is everything

We were made to receive love, and we have. Every day we should thank God for the love we have already known, for the love that has made us who we are, the love that has shown us what is truly important in life. We need to thank the Lord for the love we have received from our families, our friends, our teachers, and all those people in our lives who have helped us to realize how precious we are, in their eyes and in the eyes of God.

Do not be afraid to choose love

We were also made to give love, to make love it the inspiration for all we do and the most enduring thing in our lives. At times this seems so natural, especially when we feel the exhilaration of love, when our hearts brim over with generosity, idealism, the desire to help others, to build a better world. But at other times we realize that it is difficult to love; our hearts can easily be hardened by selfishness, envy and pride. Blessed Mother Teresa of Calcutta, the great Missionary of Charity, reminded us that giving love, pure and generous love, is the fruit of a daily decision. Every day we have to choose to love, and this requires help, the help that comes from Christ, from prayer and from the wisdom found in his word, and from the grace which he bestows on us in the sacraments of his Church.

Where is the source of love?

This is the message I want to share with you today. I ask you to look into your hearts each day to find the source of all true love. Jesus is always there, quietly waiting for us to be still with him and to hear his voice. Deep within your heart, he is calling you to spend time with him in prayer. But this kind of prayer, real prayer, requires discipline; it requires making time for moments of silence every day. Often it means waiting for the Lord to speak. Even amid the "busy-ness" and the stress of our daily lives, we need to make space for silence, because it is in silence that we find God, and in silence that we discover our true self. And in discovering our true self, we discover the particular vocation which God has given us for the building up of his Church and the redemption of our world.

Build a civilisation of love

Heart speaks unto heart. With these words from my heart, dear young friends, I assure you of my prayers for you, that your lives will bear abundant fruit for the growth of the civilization of love. I ask you also to pray for me, for my ministry as the

Successor of Peter, and for the needs of the Church throughout the world. Upon you, your families and your friends, I cordially invoke God's blessings of wisdom, joy and peace.

Radiate Christ's love to all

This is an evening of joy, of immense spiritual joy, for all of us. A great son of this nation, Cardinal John Henry Newman, will be declared Blessed. How many people, in England and throughout the world, have longed for this moment! It is also a great joy for me, personally, to share this experience with you. As you know, Newman has long been an important influence in my own life and thought, as he has been for so many people beyond these isles. The drama of Newman's life invites us to examine our lives, to see them against the vast horizon of God's plan, and to grow in communion with the Church of every time and place: the Church of the apostles, the Church of the martyrs, the Church of the saints, the Church which Newman loved and to whose mission he devoted his entire life.

Relevance of Newman today

I am especially pleased to see the many young people who are present for this vigil. This evening, in the context of our common prayer, I would like to reflect with you about a few aspects of Newman's life which I consider very relevant to our lives as believers and to the life of the Church today.

We are made to know the truth

Let me begin by recalling that Newman, by his own account, traced the course of his whole life back to a powerful experience of conversion which he had as a young man. It was an immediate experience of the truth of God's word, of the objective reality of Christian revelation as handed down in the Church. This experience, at once religious and intellectual, would inspire his vocation to be a minister of the Gospel, his discernment of the source of authoritative teaching in the Church of God, and his zeal for the renewal of ecclesial life in fidelity to the apostolic tradition. At the end of his life, Newman would describe his life's work as a struggle against the growing tendency to view religion as a purely private and subjective matter, a question of personal opinion. Here is the first lesson we can learn from his life: in our day, when an intellectual and moral relativism threatens to sap the very foundations of our society, Newman reminds us that, as men and women made in the image and likeness of God, we were created to know the truth, to find in that truth our ultimate freedom and the fulfilment of our deepest human aspirations. In a word, we are meant to know Christ, who is himself "the way, and the truth, and the life" (*Jn* 14:6).

Genuine conversion costs

Newman's life also teaches us that passion for the truth, intellectual honesty and genuine conversion are costly. The truth that sets us free cannot be kept to ourselves; it calls for testimony, it begs to be heard, and in the end its convincing power comes from itself and not from the human eloquence or arguments in which it may be couched. Not far from here, at Tyburn, great numbers of our brothers and sisters died for the faith; the witness of their fidelity to the end was ever more powerful than the inspired words that so many of them spoke before surrendering everything to the Lord. In our own time, the price to be paid for fidelity to the Gospel is no longer being hanged, drawn and quartered but it often involves being dismissed out of hand, ridiculed or parodied. And yet, the Church cannot withdraw from the task of proclaiming Christ and his Gospel as saving truth, the source of our ultimate happiness as individuals and as the foundation of a just and humane society.

Witnesses must live out their faith

Finally, Newman teaches us that if we have accepted the truth of Christ and committed our lives to him, there can be no separation between what we believe and the way we live our lives. Our every thought, word and action must be directed to the glory of God and the spread of his Kingdom. Newman understood this, and was the great champion of the prophetic office of the Christian laity. He saw clearly that we do not so much accept the truth in a purely intellectual act as embrace it in a spiritual dynamic that penetrates to the core of our being. Truth is passed on not merely by formal teaching, important as that is, but also by the witness of lives lived in integrity, fidelity and holiness; those who live in and by the truth instinctively recognize what is false and, precisely as false, inimical to the beauty and goodness which accompany the splendour of truth, *veritatis splendor*.

You must radiate the love of Christ

Tonight's first reading is the magnificent prayer in which Saint Paul asks that we be granted to know "the love of Christ which surpasses all understanding" (*Eph* 3:14-21). The Apostle prays that Christ may dwell in our hearts through faith (cf. *Eph* 3:17) and that we may come to "grasp, with all the saints, the breadth and the length, the height and the depth" of that love. Through faith we come to see God's word as a lamp for our steps and light for our path (cf. *Ps* 119:105). Newman, like the countless saints who preceded him along the path of Christian discipleship, taught that the "kindly light" of faith leads us to realize the truth about ourselves, our dignity as God's children, and the sublime destiny which awaits us in heaven. By letting the light of faith shine in our hearts, and by abiding in that light through our daily union with the Lord in prayer and participation in the life-giving sacraments of the Church, we ourselves become light to those around us; we exercise our "prophetic office"; often, without even knowing it, we draw people one step closer to the Lord and his truth. Without the life of prayer, without the interior transformation which takes place through the grace of the sacraments, we cannot, in Newman's words, "radiate Christ"; we become just another "clashing cymbal" (1 *Cor* 13:1) in a world filled with growing noise and confusion, filled with false paths leading only to heartbreak and illusion.

What is Christ asking of you?

One of the Cardinal's best-loved meditations includes the words, "God has created me to do him some definite service. He has committed some work to me which he has not committed to another" (*Meditations on Christian Doctrine*). Here we see Newman's fine Christian realism, the point at which faith and life inevitably intersect. Faith is meant to bear fruit in the transformation of our world through the power of the Holy Spirit at work in the lives and activity of believers. No one who looks realistically at our world today could think that Christians can afford to go on with business as usual, ignoring the profound crisis of faith which has overtaken our society, or simply trusting that the patrimony of values handed down by the Christian centuries will continue to inspire and shape the future of our society. We know that in times of crisis and upheaval God has raised up great saints and prophets for the renewal of the Church and Christian society; we trust in his providence and we pray for his continued guidance. But each of us, in accordance with his or her state of life, is called to work for the advancement of God's Kingdom by imbuing temporal life with the values of the Gospel. Each of us has a mission; each of us is called to change the world, to work for a culture of life, a culture forged by love and respect for the dignity of each human person. As our Lord tells us in the Gospel we have just heard, our light must shine in the sight of all, so that, seeing our good works, they may give praise to our heavenly Father (cf. *Mt* 5:16).

What definite service has God for you?

Here I wish to say a special word to the many young people present. Dear young friends: only Jesus knows what "definite service" he has in mind for you. Be open to his voice resounding in the depths of your heart: even now his heart is speaking to your heart. Christ has need of families to remind the world of the dignity of human love and the beauty of family life. He needs men and women who devote their lives to the noble task of education, tending the young and forming them in the ways of the Gospel. He needs those who will consecrate their lives to the pursuit of perfect charity, following him in chastity, poverty and obedience, and serving him in the least of our brothers and sisters. He needs the powerful love of contemplative religious, who sustain the Church's witness and activity through their constant prayer. And he needs priests, good and holy priests, men who are willing to lay down their lives for their sheep. Ask our Lord what he has in mind for you! Ask him for the generosity to say "yes!" Do not be afraid to give yourself totally to Jesus. He will give you the grace you need to fulfil your vocation.

Pray for help and illumination

And now, dear friends, let us continue our vigil of prayer by preparing to encounter Christ, present among us in the Blessed Sacrament of the Altar. Together, in the silence of our common adoration, let us open our minds and hearts to his presence, his love, and the convincing power of his truth. In a special way, let us thank him for the enduring witness to that truth offered by Cardinal John Henry Newman. Trusting in his prayers, let us ask the Lord to illumine our path, and the path of all British society, with the kindly light of his truth, his love and his peace. Amen.

Making the best of school and study

People often tell us our schooldays are the best time of our lives, but we may not be so sure. We probably do realize that school is for our benefit. It's important to appreciate that school is valuable: it's a time when we acquire knowledge, skills, wisdom, and wider interests for our future. It's a time when we develop character and personality, and learn values that can help us become mature, confident and successful in personal relationships for the rest of our lives, whatever God has in store for us - marriage, parenthood, priesthood or religious life.

Developing our abilities

Each one of us is different, and uniquely precious in God's eyes. We should allow our talents to grow by doing the best we can. Everything we learn can be useful in developing those talents: in study, sports, music, acting, whatever. It's essential that we develop our natural ability to distinguish between true and false, between good and bad. We all of us need to learn to make right choices, to appreciate what is worthwhile, and to take nothing for granted. When we have to study, we might prefer to be doing something else, but when a particular task is finished we'll be pleased we kept at it.

Jesus helps us

There are times when we will be confused, feel under a lot of pressure, feel a bit lost or lose interest. Peer pressure can be tough, and sometimes it's easier to be 'cool' than to be considered a 'geek'. Growing up and going through school is not always easy – for anyone - no matter what people say. We need good friends, and we also need to know we can turn to God. In Jesus, God shows us we can face up to problems, no matter how big or impossible they may seem, and not be destroyed by them; in fact the opposite: with his help we discover life and strength through our problems.

Our faith is part of our education

Remember, we human beings instinctively want to find the truth and, in this search, science, arts and religion are our guides. We have not only a mind, but also a spirit, and as we are educated, these develop hand in hand. We cannot truly understand the world we are growing up in without referring to God, and if we exclude our Christian faith from our learning we risk living meaningless lives, lives without hope. The brain we have been given also helps us understand religious and moral principles, common sense and a decent code of conduct. We come face to face not just with something great but with Someone great, Our Lord Jesus Christ. He has given us our skills and talents, and the opportunity to nurture and develop them, and thus serve God and our neighbour. Do not underestimate your importance and value to God, and to the Christian community.

Some tips about studying

- *Don't panic*: when you have a homework or coursework assignment, don't feel isolated or bewildered.

- *Be sure*: make sure you know what is required. If you're not sure, ask your teacher. Whatever you may think of your teachers, their job is to help develop your intelligence and emotional nature so that, eventually, you can work out the answers for yourself.

- *Help is OK*: you'll also find your parents more able to help than you think, especially if you ask at a convenient moment.

- *Don't delay*: we only make more work for ourselves by leaving things to the last minute, or attempting assignments at the worst possible time.

- *Start now*: when you get home you want to use the computer, watch TV, listen to music, or just relax. But at the back of your mind is an uneasy feeling it would have been better if the work had come first. So set yourself a routine.

- *Make a plan*: work out exactly what you need to do, and maybe make a list. Any task is more daunting when it's undefined; name it, and it becomes concrete and manageable.

- *Choose a place*: gather everything you need beforehand, and have some tidiness and quiet as you work. Try turning off the radio (and the TV) to see if this helps you concentrate.

- *Remember*: God is close to us, and we are always in his presence.

Daily study prayer

Lord, you are my strength and my guide. Grant me wisdom and understanding. Help me to do the best I can, and to enjoy this day you have given me. Help me to be kind and considerate to the people you send into my life, and not to give up if things seem difficult. Amen.

Turn to the Saints

The saints in heaven want to help us. Don't hesitate to ask them for inspiration. First, think of your own patron saint whose name you received in Baptism, and say a short prayer to him or her. Then there is your Guardian Angel, charged by God with protecting you. If you're having problems or worries, there may be a saint who experienced the same who you can ask for help.

If you're finding study difficult, ask St Joseph of Cupertino. He was hopelessly stupid at school but learned to do the best he could and leave the rest to God.

If you're being bullied, ask St Damien of Molokai. He was mocked because of his accent and because he didn't speak the language properly, but stood up against school bullies.

If you're worried about being popular, and are tempted to change to fit in, ask Blessed Pier Giorgio Frassati. He was very popular, but wouldn't compromise. He joined in all the games and sports, but went to Mass daily and made no secret of his faith.

If you're embarrassed about being a good student, ask St Gabriel Possenti or St Catherine of Alexandria. St Gabriel is the patron of Catholic youth. He was brilliant at school and also brave without being boastful. He once singlehandedly saved a whole village from bandits. St Catherine was another brilliant student who once beat a whole crowd of pagan philosophers in a public debate. She is also the only saint to have a firework named after her.

If you know you've been bad, and want to change, ask St Augustine. He was a rebel and enjoyed doing wrong. He joined a pagan cult and his life was a mess; but eventually he became the most famous Bishop in Christendom and wrote books we still read today.

If you're being judged for your appearance, ask St Thomas Aquinas. He was fat and seemed slow to learn, but became one of the Church's finest thinkers.

If you spend too much time playing computer games, or thinking about clothes, ask St Ignatius Loyola. He was addicted to trashy novels, fashionable clothes, and daydreaming; but after he was wounded in a battle, he turned to Jesus Christ, went to university, and started the Jesuits, a famous order of missionaries.

St Thomas Aquinas

A famous theologian, Thomas Aquinas (his surname means "from Aquino", his birthplace) was the son of an Italian nobleman. He became a member of the Dominican Order (Order of Preachers), and died in 1274 aged about fifty. Although he seemed a slow learner at first (he was fat, and habitually silent, and so was nicknamed the "dumb ox"), his teachers eventually realized he was an enormously talented theologian; he was also a man of deep prayer. He is best known for his voluminous writings, which include theological works, commentaries on Scripture, and some well-known prayers and hymns. His most famous work is the *Summa Theologiae* (Compendium of Theology), a systematic treatise covering the whole of Christian theology, which was a standard textbook until the 1960s. He was declared a Doctor of the Church in 1567. He is often considered a patron saint of study, and of education in general.

Prayers to St Thomas Aquinas

- You experienced the mockery and misunderstanding of others; teach us to bear with patience, as you did, those times we receive the scorn or ridicule of others.

- Those who noticed only your body were surprised to learn of the great knowledge of and love for God it concealed; help us not to judge others by outward appearance, but to remember that all men and women are made in God's image and likeness.

- You gave glory to God by your writing and thought; help us to place all the works of our hands and minds at the service of God and His Church.

- You delighted to teach, and to learn; teach us to know and love God as you did, and to recognize in all we experience the signs of his overwhelming love for us.

We pray especially for [*add your intention*] - *Our Father – Hail Mary – Glory Be*.

St Josephine Bakhita

Josephine Bakhita was born in Sudan in around 1869 but was abducted by slave traders at a young age and was so traumatized she forgot her own name.  She is known by the cynical name given to her by her abductors – Bakhita, which means "Lucky". Bakhita was passed around from "owner" to "owner" and one of them had her body scarred with intricate patterns. Eventually she ended up with an Italian family who sent her to school with the Canossian sisters in Schio, Venice. There she was baptized Josephine. Contrary to the wishes of the family, she remained with the Canossians and became a religious. She was the doorkeeper of the order and was well loved by the local people for her deep compassion and sweetness which she didn't lose even during the long, painful illness which preceded her death. Josephine Bakhita was canonized in 2000.

Prayers to St Josephine Bakhita

- St Josephine, you were taken from your family at an early age and lost your entire identity. We pray for all those children who have been abducted and for their parents and families who suffer not knowing what has become of them. Send your Holy Spirit to comfort them; and may they one day be reunited.

- You knew what it was to be a slave, to have no rights, to have lost even your name. We pray for the victims of people traffickers and all those in any kind of slavery. May this evil be wiped out from our world.

- Even in the terrible suffering of your life, you saw beauty in the world and believed there must be a God because of that beauty. May we too have something of your love for beauty and the natural world.

- Your sufferings gave you great compassion for others and you were constantly smiling and always open to those who came to you, no matter how inconvenient it was. St Josephine, may we have something of your sweetness and openness, something of your joy.

We pray especially for [*add your intention*] - *Our Father – Hail Mary – Glory Be.*

St Damien of Molokai

Damien de Veuster was born in Belgium in 1840 into a Flemish-speaking family of grain merchants. His parents wanted him to go into the family business but when he wanted to join the Congregation of the Sacred Hearts of Jesus and  Mary, like his older brother, they did not stand in his way. Damien's older brother was meant to go to Hawaii to the missions, but when he became ill Damien arranged to take his place. Once ordained and given his own parish, Damien was full of energy – evangelizing, building churches, farming, ministering to his parishioners, and debunking voodoo. Later he volunteered to be the resident priest on Molokai, a horrific leper colony, where he set about the physical and spiritual care of the sufferers, changing their lives until he himself died of the disease sixteen years later. He was only forty-nine. He was beatified in 1995 and canonized in 2009. He is considered patron of those with leprosy, those suffering from HIV/AIDS, and all those cast out by society. He is also patron of the American state of Hawaii.

Prayers to St Damien of Molokai

- You were sent away to school in a region where you didn't speak the language and people tried to bully you because of it. We pray for those who are bullied whether at school or at work or in whatever situation. May they emulate you in not accepting it.

- You loved your parents but you loved God more. You knew God was calling you to the priesthood and you answered that call although you knew your parents had other hopes of you. May we put God first and never refuse his call because of any other attachment.

- You gave up family, country and language to go and evangelize, knowing that you would never see your home or family again. Accord us something of your courage and clear-sightedness.

- When you went to Molokai you were prepared to give up your life to serve others. Help us to understand this Christian love and to begin to desire it for ourselves.

- You suffered greatly on Molokai because you were cut off from the sacraments, especially the sacrament of reconciliation. May we understand the importance of this sacrament and have recourse to it often.

- You suffered terrible loneliness and turned to the Blessed Sacrament for comfort. We pray for all who are lonely. Help us to give time to anyone we know who is lonely, and to give time to Christ in the Blessed Sacrament.

We pray especially for [*add your intention*] - *Our Father – Hail Mary – Glory Be.*

Prayer to St Rita

Rita Lotti was born to elderly parents near Cascia, in the Italian region of Umbria, around 1381. She wanted to join the convent and become a nun, but

instead obeyed her parents and got married. Her marriage was a difficult one and her husband was eventually killed in a vendetta. When her sons planned to avenge their father, Rita prayed that they wouldn't commit murder, even if it meant they die first. Both of them died from illness soon afterwards. Rita then tried to enter the convent, but the community was reluctant to take her. She did not give up, and waited for God to make it possible. In the meantime, she brokered peace between her husband's family and that of his murderer, thus ending the vendetta. Finally she was accepted into the convent.

One day, when she was praying for a share in Christ's sufferings, a thorn from Christ's crown of thorns pierced her forehead. She suffered the pain of the resulting suppurating wound for the rest of her life. She is known to be effective in making peace, especially in families, and is called the saint of things despaired of.

Prayers to St Rita

- You wanted the best for your sons even if it meant their death. Help all mothers of difficult children to pray for them, and to entrust them to God's providence and mercy.

- You brokered peace between your husband's family and the family of his murderer. We ask you to intercede anywhere in our lives there is discord and hatred.

- You did everything God asked of you, but he didn't give you your heart's desire. Help us not to become bitter if God has not rewarded us as we think we deserve. May we humbly ask his will.

- You persevered in your desire to enter the convent, waiting on God's time. Eventually everything became easy and you were able to enter. Help us to persevere in prayer for our intentions and trustingly accept God's will whatever the outcome.

- You were famed for your compassion and wisdom and many people came to ask your help. Intercede for us that we can be open to others.

We pray especially for [*add your intention*] - *Our Father – Hail Mary – Glory Be*.

St Thomas More

Thomas More was born in London in 1478. He married and had four children and after the death of his first wife married again. More was a devoted

father who made sure his daughters were educated as well as his son - unusual in those days. He was also very successful in his career, being a lawyer, then a judge known for his fairness and incorruptibility and finally becoming Lord Chancellor. As well as this he was a theologian, author and personal friend of the king. But when he had to choose between all of this and faith, he chose faith, entering into the consequences of that with his eyes wide open. He could not in conscience say that Henry VIII's marriage to Catherine of Aragon was not valid, or that the King was head of the Church in England, and he was imprisoned and executed for treason because of this. He was canonized in 1935 and shares a feast day with St John Fisher, a bishop martyred for the same reasons. He is often seen as patron of politicians and all those in public life, and of all trying to live Christian lives in the world.

Prayers to St Thomas More

- You were successful in your career, but were also known for your integrity. Intercede for us that we may be honest and hard-working in our professions.

- You were well known for your sense of humour and love of life. You were even able to make jokes on the scaffold. Intercede for us that we may learn truly to enjoy life and to learn how to be happy in all situations.

- You knew your faith and learned how to defend it. Help us to learn to do the same, so that we can have a solid foundation on which to base our lives and a way of passing the Gospel to others.

- You were not afraid to be the lone voice of truth even when you knew it could cost you everything. Intercede for us that we may be able to stand up for the teachings of the Church even when they are unpopular.

- You were finally betrayed by someone you had helped. May we too learn to forgive those who have betrayed our trust.

- You went to your death in the sure hope of eternal life. Give us too something of your faith, your hope and your courage.

We pray especially for [*add your intention*] - *Our Father – Hail Mary – Glory Be.*

St Martha

St Martha lived with her brother Lazarus and sister Mary in Bethany. Jesus often visited them there.

 Martha was the one who looked after the house, and is therefore the patron of cooks and homemakers. The Gospels record an incident where Martha complained to Jesus that he had not told her sister Mary to help her with serving their guests, but let her sit and listen to him. Jesus told Martha not to worry about so many things; and that her sister was right to put listening to him first.

Martha later recognized Jesus as the Messiah, and witnessed him raise her brother Lazarus from the dead. After the Resurrection of Jesus, it is said that she and her brother and sister evangelized in France, where Martha converted many people through her preaching, calling them away from the worship of a dragon god.

Prayers to St Martha

- Yours was a home that Christ himself was comfortable in. We ask you help us to be hospitable and open and to make our homes a place where Christ can be present.

- You worked hard in your house. Help us to give value to housework and the routine tasks of life. Intercede for us so that we can look after others' needs with serenity and joy.

- Help us to work for the good of others, but always to put Christ first. Help us also to learn from Christ, as you did, not to worry and fret, but to trust in God's all-powerful providence.

- The Lord rebuked you for your judgement, anger and self importance and you accepted it. You knew he loved you. We ask that we may be able to accept criticism without remaining resentful and without being destroyed by it.

- You saw Christ raise your brother from the dead. Intercede for us so our eyes can be opened to the miracles Christ has done in our lives.

We pray especially for [*add your intention*] - *Our Father – Hail Mary – Glory Be.*

St Joseph of Cupertino

Because his father had died leaving debts and his family was consequently homeless, Joseph Desa was an unwelcome addition when he was born in Cupertino, Italy in 1603. As a child he was slow witted and had a habit of standing with his mouth open staring into space. He also had a terrible temper, probably born of frustration. Even his own mother thought him worthless. As a young man he joined the Capuchins but was sent away because the ecstasies he experienced made him unsuitable for work. Finally he was accepted by the Franciscans who, seeing his holiness, put him forward to train for the priesthood. Joseph was so unintelligent that the best he could do was to study a small portion of the material he was supposed to know, and then pray that that's what he would be asked. Whilst with the Franciscans he began to levitate in ecstasy at the mention of any holy thing and only a command from his superior could bring him to earth. Joseph was investigated (and exonerated) by the Inquisition because of his antigravitational activities. This also caused his superiors to move him into seclusion. He had his own room and chapel and was unable to leave them. Often those in charge even forgot to bring him food but he accepted everything with humility. He died a holy death aged sixty. He is a patron of students doing exams and of air travellers.

Prayers to St Joseph of Cupertino

- You were an unwanted child and were thought worthless even by your own mother. Intercede for all unwanted children that they may come to know they were born out of God's love for them.

- You were an angry, frustrated child. We pray for all who struggle to express themselves, and that you help us overcome sins of anger.

- You experienced no love in your family and were considered of little account by all who knew you. We pray for all who have experienced the same. May we learn to treat everyone as having the worth they have in God's eyes.

- You suffered because of your lack of intelligence. We pray for all those who struggle at school. May they take comfort from the fact that lack of intelligence didn't stop you becoming a saint.

- You did the best with the little intelligence you had, and put the rest in God's hands. That way you passed all your exams and became a priest. We pray for all those struggling with exams. May we also do our best in everything and trust in God to guide our lives.

- You were unjustly suspected, investigated, confined to your room and neglected by those charged with looking after you. You accepted all this with humility. We pray for all those unjustly imprisoned, and that we too may have the humility to accept injustice for the love of Christ.

We pray especially for [*add your intention*] - *Our Father – Hail Mary – Glory Be.*